Conflict as Choice

*"Out beyond the ideas of right and wrong doing,
there is a field. I'll meet you there."*
— JELALUDDIN RUMI

Praise for "Life Without Conflict"

"Life Without Conflict *serves the important purpose of reminding all of us,
irrespective of our unique backgrounds and careers, to recognize that while
conflicts are inevitable, we have choices to make when we encounter them.
The authors have written a practical, concise guide that will be helpful to
those who want to do a better job of taking charge of their lives."*
— DR. DAVID CAMPBELL
A Nationally-Recognized
Superintendent of Schools

*"Gerber and Leech provide the essential tools for moving our lives
and organizations beyond conflict and toward interest-based,
win-win solutions – 'by merely choosing to do so.' "*
— CARRIE JACOBS, PhD, LSW
Executive Director
The Attic Youth Center

"Conflict is the beginning of consciousness."
— M. ESTHER HARDING

Life without Conflict

INTRODUCTION TO A WINNING LIFE

Published by Timeless Publishing
www.Timelesspublishing.com

Library of Congress Control Number: 2006907299
ISBN 0-9788707-0-0

Printed in the United States of America

Special thanks for our Cover Layout
Designed by Robert Allan & Associates

Special thanks to Gaye Newton for her editing support

Acknowledgements

*"Sometimes our light goes out but is blown
into flame by another human being.
Each of us owes deepest **thanks** to those
who have rekindled this light."*
— ALBERT SCHWEITZER

I would like to give my deepest recognition, love and acknowledgement to Kakki and Jessie, who have made sacrifices and have enabled me to give my all to this project. Thank you to my parents, brother and grandparents, for their ongoing guidance and support. Also, to a great friend, Gary Cook, who has inspired me with his strength and love of life. Thank you for the lessons learned that have been transformed into this work and for encouraging me at the most difficult of hours. — DAVE GERBER

First and foremost, I would like to say a very big "thank you" to my husband, Michael, who stands by me all the time, with support and love; "thank you" to my Mother, Edith, my constant companion since birth who models spirit and compassion in my world; to my stepdaughter, Michele, who gives me the joy of motherhood, and to my spiritual mentor, Daisaku Ikeda, who on a daily basis models, how to achieve a happy life and world peace. Less specifically, but equally important, I would like to say "thank you" to every human being I have had the pleasure to meet, for all have been on my path to insure my understanding of the most exquisite jewel of all – LIFE! — PAMELA LEECH

*"I would maintain that **thanks** are the highest form of thought,
and that gratitude is happiness doubled by wonder."*
— G.K. CHESTERTON

Table of Contents

Purpose

"The truth is that our finest moments are most likely to occur when we are feeling deeply uncomfortable, unhappy, or unfulfilled. For it is only in such moments, propelled by our discomfort, that we are likely to step out of our ruts and start searching for different ways or truer answers."
— M. SCOTT PECK

What is our purpose for writing?

It is our goal to help individuals increase their own conflict fluency in order to become more comfortable confronting, addressing, using and moving beyond a state of conflict by merely choosing to do so.

Developing this book has allowed us to work through our own issues — and those of friends and clients — and use those experiences within our respective practices. The result is some insightful tools that are immediately applicable to every human being.

"You can come to understand your purpose in life by slowing down and feeling your heart's desires."
— MARCIA WIEDER

INTRODUCTION TO A WINNING LIFE

Preface

*"The torment of human frustration, whatever its immediate cause,
is the knowledge that the self is in prison, its vital force and 'mangled mind'
leaking away in lonely, wasteful self-conflict."*
– ELIZABETH DREW

Why read this booklet?

Read this booklet to help move beyond the basic human elements of conflict that keep us from expanding upon our potential and from finding the happiness we deserve.

Quite often, before real life change becomes the number one objective, we must hit some level of discomfort in our personal and/or professional life that we find unacceptable. Some may need to sink to their perceived lowest level of motivation, job or family satisfaction. Others may be putting up with some old discomforts they have become accustomed to feeling. Wherever we lie on that continuum, we can always improve our lives and happiness by learning to overcome obstacles that will inherently surface in every day living.

Do we ever get comfortable being numb or satisfied with the pain because the work ahead seems daunting, overwhelming and, in some way, not worth it? Do our issues of fear, anger, control and more ever dictate our daily attitude, moods, self-esteem and vision for the future?

Whether we have been there or not, rock bottom or truly feeling that life can offer us more, one constant generally appears—the desire to feel alive! To do this, we must develop a condition of life, a state of clarity that is not swayed by life's changes. This is a life of hope, possibility and learning versus doom, problems and perceived failures.

We have free will. We can choose our own reality and choose to live each moment as it if were our last, refusing to be limited by past fears and guilt. Once we become conscious of how we feel, we make choices. We can let go of anticipated realities we make up that predetermine an unfulfilling future. When peace of mind is our single most important focus, we can create and find our happiness—literally, our inner peace.

"A man who dares to waste an hour of time
has not discovered the value of life."
– CHARLES DARWIN

*"The art and science of asking questions
is the source of all knowledge."*
– THOMAS BERGER

I.

Essential Conflict Questions

When we take the time to slow down, listen and learn, we often find that our desire to seek grows stronger than our fear of being wrong. The following are 13 Essential Questions that will get to the heart of conflict-related issues. These are the stake in the ground for our exploration throughout this text. To that end, further answers to these questions will be explored in greater detail and from different perspectives.

1. What is conflict?

The World Reference Encyclopedia gives many examples of conflict such as a struggle, or fight, battle, dispute, difference, or an "opposition between two simultaneous but incompatible feelings", or a "state of opposition between persons or ideas or interests."[1] That said, it is obvious why our society sees conflict as an obstacle, not an opportunity for closure or growth. We will explore the positives and negatives of conflict.

Conflict is a state of mind determined by choice. That choice is how we react to what other people say or do. Many people choose to engage in or escalate conflict, rather than move slowly and make decisions based on the outcomes they want. Some people can even become "emotionally hijacked," a changing physiological state where blood pressure increases and chemicals are released in the brain causing us to feel differently.

When you have a panic attack, or become very anxious your emotional response can actually bypass your 'thinking brain'. The…amygdale [small but powerful part of the brain], which is involved with creating a 'faster than thought' panic attack… [gets triggered]. It is very difficult, or impossible, to think clearly when highly emotional because the part of the brain you think with is inhibited…This response has been termed an "emotional hijacking" by Daniel Goleman.[2]

Our brains are hardwired, unfortunately, in a primitive way to protect ourselves. An analogy would be that our brains were programmed for conflict, and therefore our physical body would change, as well, when we saw a saber tooth tiger.

While there are no more saber tooth tigers today, conflict stimulates our programmed, primitive response in a similar way it did thousands of years ago. Similar to the past, these situations ignite those body and mind changes we seem to have to work very hard to control, if possible.

Conflict has often been framed as Man vs. Man, Man vs. Nature, and Man vs. Self. Here we will focus on conflict within oneself. Whether internal conflict represents an immediate, in-your-face or an ongoing situation, it affects who we are—the very core of our being, the person we speak to when we talk to ourselves. Not surprisingly, much of our self talk is negative. Our focus is on the underlying levels of personal conflict that play out during these frustrating, isolated experiences and the experience itself.

How do these feelings and emotions change us and impact those around us? How often do we treat strangers better than our loved ones, friends or acquaintances?

Conflict often happens when roadblocks appear, when we fixate on our positions instead of interests, when we lack the desire to understand before we are understood, when we believe that our perception is the only one, when we refuse to be active listeners, when we allow our inner child to dominate. Such conflicts—usually based on our issues of fear, anger, control, shame and guilt—create win-lose situations.

We have a societal tendency to view conflict as negative. However, conflict may be absolutely necessary for people to move forward together. To illustrate the point, imagine a 20-pound bag of potatoes. As the bag is transported, the potatoes bang up against each other. If there's too much force, they end up damaged and no longer useful. But with the right amount of jostling, they come out clean.

Remember a time when we did not experience conflict? If we are honest with ourselves, the answer is usually no. From the beginning of our lives, screaming and crying was our only way to tell everyone that something in our world wasn't right. We were in conflict with our dirty diaper, a hungry belly, lack of warmth or attention, or sometimes pain. Conflict is a human phenomenon, a part of both the nature and nurture cycles. We may have a larger vocabulary, a louder voice, and bigger temper than our younger selves, but in reality, conflict has been a constant in our lives.

2. Is conflict positive or negative?

It's both. As we alluded, conflict can do a number of things. Positive conflict will often be the only way to proactively deal with issues that people or groups need to have addressed. Conflict can be the beginning to any great thing or the ending of something that needs closure.

Like all phenomena in the universe, conflict is both good and bad, yin and yang, so to speak. As Paramahansa Yogananda, an Indian Yogi, said, "There are always two forces warring against each other within us."

Positive conflict can:
- Be the start to something new
- Initiate change
- Be the end to something that needs closure
- Positively redirect something off track
- Use diversity
- Promote understanding
- Support dialogue
- Enlighten someone that is unaware of a problem
- Be the start of something unexpected
- Become a life-long learning opportunity
- Foster self-esteem
- Reinforce our current abilities, strengths or contributions
- Help work to ensure life-long happiness

But remember, just because it is positive does not mean that it will be easy or painless.

Negative conflict can:
- Create more conflict
- Eliminate "Response Ability"
- Create physiological responses that impede our ability to make sound, cognitive, logical decisions
- Sabotage decision making
- Undermine creativity
- Re-emphasize our past poor decision making
- Trigger our default behavior that creates more conflict
- Cause anxiety, mental and physical stress and/or sickness
- Annihilate respect and trust
- Impede our ability to move forward internally or with others
- Create war

As previously mentioned, positive conflict, by its very nature, can signal a moment to explore perspectives, look at common interests, open lines of communication, generate learning opportunities and help us to separate the people from the problem.

We far too often see people react to conflict negatively with anger, avoidance, fear, guilt, shame, procrastination or complete shut down. But it is equally possible for individuals to choose positive thinking, to brainstorm and produce new perspectives, ideas and even a new road map or new dynamic. The process can strengthen character and reinforce how we view and ultimately use conflict to our advantage.

3. How does perception play into conflict issues?

Our perception is our reality. When something happens, we attach our own personal interpretation to the event, often without hesitation. Like it or not, this perspective is a bias, the effect of our collective, real and imagined life experiences. If our perception is reality, simply, everyone in society is operating under the rules of the reality they have established. Someone once alluded that the only false perception is the one that claims to be the only perception that exists at all.

When conflict happens and we look at a situation, one way to begin the diffusion process is to consider someone else's perspective, even if they are not involved in the situation. How might she or he see it differently? How can our ability to look from another perspective impact our ability to shift the dynamic and find temporary or permanent solutions?

4. How can conflict be a change agent?

As we mentioned earlier, conflict can signal a moment to explore perspectives, look to common interests, open lines of communication, generate learning opportunities, separate the person from the problem and help us look at the conflict from the 10,000-foot view. We can try to understand the overall context of the situation.

Conflict as a change agent can produce a wide range of consequences. It can be extremely motivating, increase individual and/or group morale, and encourage positive risk taking. It can promote growth, understanding and personal advancement. But if we attach ourselves to the negative aspects of conflict— such as fear, anger and control—we can expect out-of-control environments, internal chaos, judgment, anger, frustration and more conflict!

5. What are individuals' typical reactions to conflict?

People respond to conflict in a variety of ways. While some are excited and see the possibilities of conflict positively channeled as a means for change, most do not. Individuals typically respond with anger, avoidance, fear, guilt, shame, positional thinking, attacks, withdrawal, procrastination, stalling or inaction. Some individuals will choose to bulldoze through conflict and others will be agreeable and do everything within their means to avoid a power struggle.

Infantile responses are not uncommon. Fear often triggers past, painful lessons that live on in our subconscious. Individuals often associate current situations with childhood pains and may have few coping skills for moving forward. But the ability to manage conflict is essential to establishing a winning life.

6. What variables should we consider when dealing with conflict?

Many variables can come into play in a conflict situation, including:

- Perception
- Realization
- Prejudice
- Socialization
- Culture
- Cultural transmission
- Values
- Fear
- Anger
- Control

- Shame
- Guilt
- Personality type
- Opinion
- Tradition
- Each person's definition of conflict
- Race
- Ethnicity
- Physiology

- Social class
- Levels of education and people's story
- Multiple intelligences
- Learning styles
- Elements of diversity
- Language and communication

And many more…

These variables earlier, what we now call life's Conflict Ingredients, are not widely taught. To that end, neither is conflict management in general. Interpersonal relationships can be delicate; it is imperative that we deeply and profoundly understand each concept.

It is often only an illusion that communication has taken place and has been effective. Communication, like the other variables listed above, is also very fragile. Communication involves elements of distance in space, time, perceptions and realities for those who are trying to understand one another. Communication can have inadvertent sub-messages that are perceived to be attached to the receiver's primary message. For instance, a message could read, "I like women," yet the sender could really mean he or she only likes a certain type of woman, without being specific. Or the receiver could imprint that same sub-message or a different one based upon the elements listed above.

An individual can also be upset with how the message was sent (i.e. in person, email, regular mail, journal, over the phone, fax, etc.). Both the method and the form of delivery can ultimately lead to both internal and external conflict.

In essence, we truly "encrypt" our messages in our own, personal version of the English language. This encryption consists of two principles;

1. The actual words selected, tone and non-verbal communication (if the communication is face to face) and

2. the method used to deliver the message, if not in person.

The recipient of our communication now has to decipher our message for content and meaning and will examine the method in which it was sent. For example, some people like to hear, "I love you," but hate it if it is only stated in an e-mail. Essentially, two people are volleying little packages of communication back and forth. Either may have a problem with the message or the type of package they receive and decode it in their own language.

Because we all speak our own version of the language, communication, particularly in the context of conflict or difficult situations, is quite fragile. Remember, communication goes well beyond what we say. Most studies on communication indicate that nonverbal behavior, tone and voice inflection play an extremely large role in the dialogue, sometimes as much or more than the actual words selected.

Conflict is not born; it is constructed and developed in a moment's notice or over a longer period of time.

7. What is the difference between conflict prevention, management and resolution?

Imagine someone trying to cover a wound with a bandage. The bleeding may stop for a brief moment with direct pressure. Could it have been easier to prevent the accident in the first place? Could that individual have chosen to wear a long sleeve shirt or a jacket, maybe some gloves before hiking through the wilderness?

Our society does not want to think about, use the energy for or spend the money to prevent conflict from happening before it starts. Consider crime. If we asked a group of parents if they would be interested in more police officers, emergency and/or fire personnel, most would say yes. If we then told them how much their taxes would need to increase to support the approved initiative, most would rationalize a way to say, "Everything is truly okay and nothing happens around here, so, no, I won't support it."

Taking the time, energy, resources and, quite often, money to prevent conflict before it starts is the only way to ensure that we are as prepared as we can be when conflict rears its head.

Human Beings = Conflict. If we believe that premise, we can believe that preventing conflict is smart and rational and will affect our professional and personal lives. Whoever said that business wasn't personal wasn't looking beyond his or her experience.

Conflict Prevention incorporates a wide range of thoughts, planning, behaviors and follow-up that creates informal and formal policies, procedures and practice, otherwise referred to as the "4 P State of Mind."

Essentially, this theory is used to describe the expectations courts of law will have on a company or organization. First, there must be policies. Secondly, we must examine the purpose of the policy in order to make sure that it is correctly stated and clear to all. Then the policies must have appropriate and clear procedures about how to follow those policies or what to do if a policy is broken. Finally, just like fire drills, procedures must be practiced. Everyone, both new hires and those who have been working for a while, needs a refresher course.

Think about it. Would it be acceptable for a school to have a fire policy but only practice it every other year? No. Policies and procedures must be put to the test and practiced. The end goal is to avert the problem or at least reduce the escalation and/or damage involved.

Conflict prevention includes:
1. Engaging in self-assessment, monitoring, and positive self-talk that will allow us to avert or manage a potentially disruptive conflict. Self-talk is widely viewed as the mini-internal discussions we have with ourselves, about our lives, during quiet times.
2. Understanding the Agents of Socialization and other root causes directly related to the conflict at hand.
3. Understanding our own buttons or default behaviors enough to warn ourselves of an impending conflict and/or a potentially harmful reaction.
4. Developing a prevention-oriented mindset that understands, anticipates and proactively considers the impact of conflict in each area of personal and professional life.

5. Ensuring ourselves and those around us that we are dedicated to strengthening our skills and preventing conflict in every aspect of life.

Conflict prevention addresses a desire to gain tools and skills that will help to ensure that negativity, or negative conflict, never happens. But this new learning is only made useful when it is applied fairly and consistently with great reflection.

Conflict Management is about using a conflict prevention mentality and working toward resolution, self-awareness and a system or procedure for immediately dealing with conflict.

Our goal is to prevent the initiation of conflict, quickly facilitate a method for containment when it happens and enable ourselves to transform the experience into solutions, calmness, growth and life-long learning.

Conflict Resolution is a method or process of extinguishing or handling a conflict, preferably quickly, by:
- Identifying the main, secondary, tertiary and related issues
- Addressing each side's (or internal competing) needs
- Adequately addressing personal and professional interests
- Investigating unmet professional expectations
- Understanding and anticipating the possible consequences of any decision (cause and effect)
- Allowing for the customized design of solutions between the parties involved in conflict
- Including all appropriate individuals and stake holders
- Staying solution oriented
- Creating a plan, making choices and confirming the outcomes
- Developing a plan for honest, effective feedback
- Actively listening to all parties involved, without interruption
- Resolving issues through arbitration, mediation, negotiation, alternative dispute resolution or a court of law

The more we focus on conflict prevention, the less conflict we will have to manage and resolve. Each of these stages is a part of the process of transforming conflict into an agent for positive change. For instance, the identification and elimination of the conditions that fuel conflict support prevention.

Management is appropriate when conflict, as positive change, is critical for achieving the desired results. Resolution encompasses prevention and management, resulting in a paradigm shift and win-win solutions for all parties involved.

8. Why should we understand the difference between positions and interests?

Stop focusing on where we are and focus on where we need and want to be when the conflict is over. Believe that a solution is possible, even if one is not clear at the moment.

As noted by Ury and Fisher in their book, Getting to Yes, positions are predetermined solutions or outcomes to a situation, conflict or problem. They represent feelings and thoughts about where we are grounded, usually only solved with a single answer, most often a discussion stopper. Interests are the underlying needs behind the positions that must be met to feel satisfaction, not necessarily victory. These represent feelings and thoughts about where we want to be and open the box for customized solutions and new conversations.[3]

Understanding and using interest-based conflict management styles in our lives will allow us to move beyond difficult situations with others. This is a beneficial and healthy transition from our old, social learning.

We believe this is one of the most important elements for individuals to capture as they move through this booklet. People often stick to their positions because they are angry, hurt, or feeling unheard. Yet these emotions get in the way of win-win solutions.

When two people enter into conflict focused on resolution that satisfies their needs, they tend to resort to protecting their positions, feelings and thoughts. But if they can focus on criteria that meet both parties' interests, the solution will be more acceptable to both.

Think of the question, "What do you need?" This is a much more forward thinking approach. Focusing on interests allows us to concentrate on why a particular solution is preferred. It generates explanations, not justification, and promotes progress toward a customized, designed and clarified win-win solution.

9. What is a lie?

We have included this as an Essential Question because we believe it is important to take responsibility for the results of our actions. Presenting false impressions can be a source of conflict. For some, it can become an endless river of fuel feeding flames of conflict draining the parties involved for years or even decades. It takes new lies to keep the old lies fresh.

Why do we lie? We often fear being judged or being put in a position where we have to justify our decisions, behaviors and comments. Remember a time when we created an impression based on information that was incomplete, reorganized or removed to change the paradigm in the head of the person with whom we were speaking with at the time?

What is a lie? We define a lie as presenting any other paradigm, regardless of how minimal the difference, than the one we believe to be true. How is information deleted, removed, reorganized to change the paradigm? How are elements of time manipulated? While these are only a few ways to manipulate the truth, it is important to investigate what our parents and extended family socialized us to believe is the truth.

Does truth mean the entire story? If details, insignificant or not, are left out, has a lie been told? Examine the definition of a lie, above, and determine whether the closest people in our lives view it the same way. If not, why? How does each person's understanding of truth impact the amount of conflict they create for themselves, internalize from the outside world, and regurgitate back into the playing field from which we work, live and spend our free time?

So, why do we lie? We often lie because we don't want conflict, we don't want to be judged nor have our desires evaluated. We don't want to feel like we have to convince the other person that our choices are appropriate. We do not want to spend the time, effort or work to make communication effective, often because we were never taught the skills. We don't want guilt, more confrontation, frustration and disagreement. We don't want conflict.

Both truth telling and lying are always about choice. One chooses to own the consequences and ripple effect that result from a false word, thought or behavior. Even if we do not want to be judged or have to justify our legitimate feelings to each other, we still make a choice when asked to tell the truth or when we are expected to fill in the details. Each conscious thought, spoken word and behavior is ultimately our own to choose and live.

10. How do we honor our personal values when managing or resolving conflict?

Values are said to be the elements in our lives that get us out of bed each day. They are the beliefs that make life worth living, whether times are good or bad. Perhaps we embrace some of the following:

Honesty • Accountability • Teamwork • Trust • Personal growth
Unconditional love • Life-long learning • Respect • Freedom
Recognition and validation • Diversity

Whatever values we currently have, do we honor them in our thoughts, words and deeds? When we are in conflict with someone, do we still honor these values that we hold true? The real question we must ask ourselves is how we choose, actively, to honor the most important values in our lives, even when things are not good.

11. What elements of diversity often cause conflict?

Most people believe they understand the concept of diversity. In reality, most only see diversity as skin color and maybe gender or sexual preference. As seen from the diagram to follow, the concept of diversity is much larger than these factors and many others not included. Why is this important? These elements represent so many human variables that often are the source of inner conflict or conflict with other people.

Examine the following diagram and imagine all of the different ways these variables can be mixed together to create one person. Is it any wonder why interpersonal relationships are difficult? Remember the last class or teacher that even came remotely close to preparing us for managing thousands of people, each with a different combination of elements, in our lifetime? Most of us were not prepared for the onslaught of people with diverse behaviors, conflict styles, and communication patterns.

Are the elements of diversity the source of our conflict, or is it our inability to understand, appreciate and use the differences for the greater good?

The Elements of Diversity within everyone!

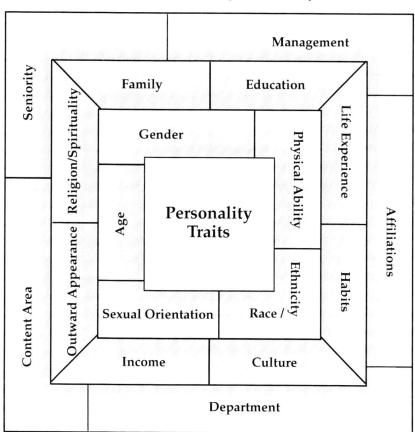

Imagine all of these variables, co-existing within every individual we try to communicate with, work with and/or love.

12. How did our parents deal with conflict and what did they teach us?

Compare the Essential Questions already explored with how we were taught to handle conflict. What do we now see and understand when we critically examine our lives?

While our parents are responsible in many ways for laying the groundwork, now that we are adults, we must make decisions for ourselves. It is neither fair nor legitimate to continue behaviors and lessons, even if unintentional, that create toxic results and unfairly perpetuate negative social learning.

After years of repetition and reinforcement, we all have incorporated early lessons into our personality. We cannot deny them or claim to be unaware. But we can still learn new, more effective behaviors. We must accept responsibility for our human transformation and recognize that we can actively make choices.

There is what we know, what we don't know, and what we don't know we don't know. Essentially, it will be up to us to select a path that empowers investigation into the personal unknown. We have the ability to make powerful choices different from those our parents and teachers made for and about us.

It is fair to say that as little children growing up we may not have been able to experience or express our emotions in ways different than those prescribed by our families? Now, as adults, we have more options, including replacing those rules with others that will truly help us move forward.

It is time for us to make our own powerful choices and harness our own power. Are we ready to step into the present? Yes? Congratulations! This is the first step forward in transforming any conflict in our lives—choice.

13. Why should we investigate this subject now?

- To improve our lives and increase internal satisfaction
- To immediately improve our personal and professional relationships
- To improve our understanding of why conflict exists and how to prevent it from happening

- To develop a stronger "conflict fluency" that will help us dissect conflict in the moment
- To help create the best solutions while in conflict as our physiology changes
- To help others in our lives reduce their conflict
- To develop more tools to deal with the quickly changing world around us
- To look at our lives from a different perspective

*"Have patience with everything that remains unsolved in your heart.
Try to love the questions themselves, like locked rooms and like books written in a foreign language. Do not now look for the answers.
They cannot now be given to you because you could not live them.
It is a question of experiencing everything. At present you need to live the question. Perhaps you will gradually, without even noticing it, find yourself experiencing the answer, some distant day."*

– RAINER MARIA RILKE

1 Wordreference.com, "Conflict," Wordreference.com, 2003,
<http://www.wordreference.com/definition/conflict/> (July 26, 2006).

2 Panic-attacks.co.uk, "Part 5: The Brain and Panic Attacks: Emotional Hijacking,"
The Panic Attack Prevention Program, 2001-2006,
<http://www.panic-attacks.co.uk/panic_attacks_5.htm /> (July 26, 2006.)

3 Robert Fischer, William Ury, and Patton, Bruce, *Getting to Yes: Negotiating Agreement without Giving In*, Penguin Group, New York, NY, 1981, 40-41

*"I know not with what weapons World War III will be fought,
but World War IV will be fought with sticks and stones."*
– ALBERT EINSTEIN

II.

Historical Conflict Timeline: Setting the Stage

Is it really any surprise that humans choose conflict as a solution to professional, personal and intimate human relationship issues? Using a socio-historical, counter productive way to solve problems, we often resort to the cave man mentality of survival of the fittest. We have modeled, taught, socialized, encouraged, praised, rewarded and even provided incentives for individuals to knowingly and unknowingly select negative conflict to deal with interpersonal relationships and encounters. Conflict has built itself into the very fabric of our society and has worked its way into our culture's collective unconscious.

A simplified dwindling road of historical conflict

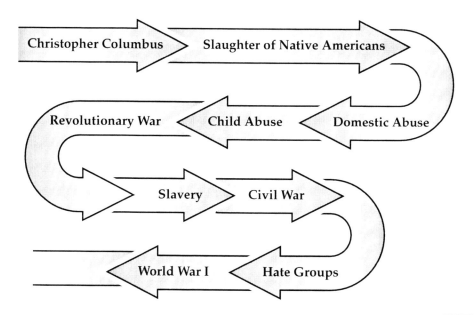

Question: What is the connection between conflict, prejudice & arrogance?

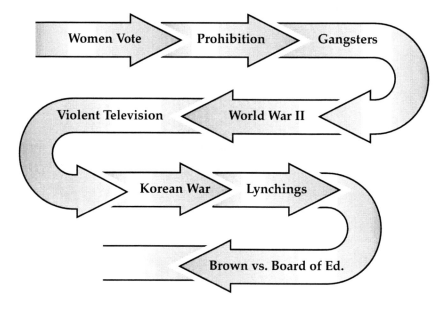

Question: What contradictory messages are characterized by individuals' conflicts of emotions, needs and values?

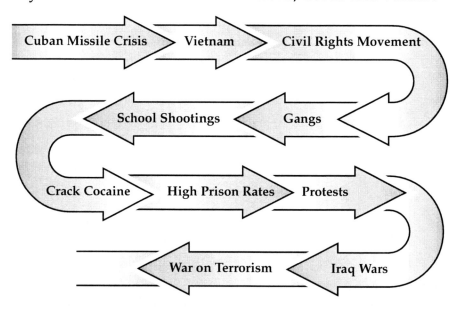

How does society feel about conflict?

AND

What conclusions can we draw about the differences between individual and group behavior?

*"Human history becomes more and more a race
between education and catastrophe."*
– H.G. WELLS

"You are what you are
because of what goes into your mind."
– ZIG ZIGLER

III.

Who is Responsible?
The Contributing Agents of Conflict

Everyone human being that inhabits the planet has responsibility. Individually we control our destiny, and collectively we manage humanity.

It is not until we become more conscious of the influences on our being that we truly understand who we are, where we came from and the society we have created and live in together. The positive, motivating, upside is that after we know this, we can take more responsibility for our decisions to engage or not engage in conflict. We can become empowered to change, to create something better.

Our society has created and passed on formal and informal standards, messages, beliefs and socialization. Early in our lives the Agents of Socialization often foster belief systems, positive and negative, that in many cases only work as theories on paper. These are often created to reduce social conflict, keep order and funnel power to the powerful.

Agents of Socialization—family, peers, school, media and religion—have affected us throughout our lives. Many of our conscious decisions are truly a product of experiences with these five agents over time, particularly from our early childhood. These Agents have all significantly influenced us since birth. A person's age, parallel life experiences and repetition of events will often gauge which Agents influence him or her at any give time. Most would consider family, particularly parents, to be the primary socialization agent (parenting styles, life lessons about behavior, values, etc). "The apple doesn't fall far from the tree."

In many ways, we are a product of what has been done to us. Social learning and lessons passed along, many with the best of intentions, have influenced all of us in almost all areas of our lives.

Consider these examples to gain more experience understanding the impact United States Agents of Socialization have on all of us and as individuals. What messages did we get (note the "?"), and how were we socialized by the Agents listed below? What messages about the topics below did we internalize from the Agents of Socialization column, and, quite possibly, pass on to a younger generation?

Replace the "?" with messages from our lives. Remember, individuals from the same and different cultures often received different messages about the same concept, group of information or set of peoples.

AGENT	#1 GENDER	#2 RACE	#3 CLASS	#4 CONFLICT
FAMILY	Ex. Men are smarter than women	?	Ex. Keeping up with the Joneses	Ex. Emotional, verbal, physical, sexual abuse
PEERS	?	Ex. Hang out with same race	?	?
MEDIA	?	?	Ex. Money buys Happiness	?
SCHOOL	Ex. Men are better at math and science	?	?	?
RELIGION	?	?	?	Ex. How are international conflicts solved

Rhetorical Questions to think about
with respect to the Agents of Socialization table.

1. Given our experiences, what's behind the question marks?

2. What subtle and obvious lessons or messages did we receive from any of the Agents?

3. What practices or beliefs do we have in our lives of which we don't know the origin? How do we play out those types of situations in our lives, anyway?

4. When we really stop and think about them, how do we perpetuate subtle or overt lessons passed along by our parents and older generations that we truly do not support?

5. Now that we understand more about the social learning that was passed along to us through cultural messages, what do we want to do with this information?

"As any action or posture long continued
will distort and disfigure the limbs;
so the mind likewise is crippled and contracted by
perpetual application to the same set of ideas."
— SAMUEL JOHNSON

*"Control your destiny or
somebody else will."*
– JACK WELSH

IV.

Internal vs. External Conflict

Internal conflict can mean feeling torn over a situation, anger or fear in response to a situation or any disruptive thing we are dealing with in our lives that distracts us from feeling good and moving forward.

We would argue that much inner conflict can be traced to unmet needs or a belief system that is driven by symbols of success (e.g., home, car, affluence, family). In fact, we have twice as many material possessions but are reported by several experts to be nearly twice as unhappy as people were in the 1950s. We consistently compare ourselves to other people, other circumstances, other results—the Joneses. This form of measurement creates suffering which promotes internal conflict.

Measuring and understanding the type, amount, source, variables and depth of internal conflict is necessary to make lasting changes. Our internal conflict may have roots in our childhood, adolescence, and young adult lives all wrapped into one. It could be anything from a situation we are dealing with now to an unmet childhood need, camouflaging and masking itself as a present pain.

Many people we have spoken with, including each other, agree that the pain we will have to go through to grow may be more intense than the discomfort we currently feel. Nevertheless, it must be experienced to grow. If we are willing to take that step, then and only then will we see things the way they really are.

If we recall the last chapter's content on the Agents of Socialization, it is much easier to see how conflict is created, transmitted, rejuvenated and often fueled as we grow older. What happens then is we affect those around us or ourselves, mentally and physically.

External Conflict

Conflict that is directed toward us may manifest as some more recognizable feeling such as irritation, envy, depression or bitterness. Actually these are all effects of a belief that presumes the outside world is the cause of our frustration. The reality is we are responsible for generating our own response (i.e., anger), as we are both the cause and the effect in any dynamic. It may be easier to avoid a situation than turn anger into calm. But in any case, we must consciously and physically decide to make that change. Both desires must come from inside.

Take a moment to remember a time when we were upset. Didn't we see the world and those in it as the reason for the upset? Conversely, consider a moment when we felt great peace of mind. To whom did we give credit for that feeling, us or the external world? We must create positive peace of mind for ourselves.

Making peace of mind our natural default or response to any circumstance is no easy accomplishment. It requires a willingness and serious commitment to change. Those who seem to find themselves in conflict often will obviously get more practice. But practice without the proper techniques only reinforces bad habits. We can't afford to strike out in the game of life for long.

External conflict is a signal that we need to consider making new choices and challenge the conflict we feel internally. We constantly struggle with what to think and how we will feel. External choice is really about internal struggle. We are the master of our minds. We can choose. In order to further explain internal and external conflict, use the following acronym, F.A.C.T.S.

"When one door of happiness closes, another opens; but often we look so hard at the closed door that we do not see the one which has opened for us."
– HELEN KELLER

V.

F.A.C.T.S.

We believe that fear, anger, control, timing and shame are the greatest inhibitors to a personal or professional life without conflict. Before explaining each concept in its own individual chapter we wanted to begin with questions for us to consider.

Use the Agents of Socialization, the Essential Questions and our experiences to explore each of these concepts and how they are directly relate to us.

F = Fear
- Would we rather use fight or flight? Why?
- What is our approach toward handling disputes or dealing with conflict?
- What are we truly, yes truly, afraid of in our lives?

A = Anger
- Who taught us to be angry?
- Who taught us what to do with our anger?
- Does anger get in our way when looking for solutions?

C = Control
- At what age did we want to be in control of our lives?
- How do we feel when someone tries to control our speech or actions?
- How do we respond when we feel as though someone is trying to control us in any way?

T = Timing
- Do we ever find it difficult to slow down during conversations? Why?
- When do we react, respond, defend or repel?

- Do we ever wish we took more time to respond during difficult or conflict situations, but are concerned about defending ourselves?

S = Shame

- "Who gave me this shame?"
- How do our shame and guilt work together?
- How do we respond to any shame we feel, ever?

F.A.C.T.S. This acronym summarizes most of the issues that act as basic life obstacles. The timing of our actions and reactions will often influence the impact of a situation. Unfortunately, most people react with conflict or behavior that brings about conflict secondarily.

"There are no facts, only interpretations."
– FRIEDRICH NIETZCHE

*"Fear is like fire: If controlled, it will help you;
if uncontrolled, it will rise up and destroy you"*
— JOHN F. MILBURN

VI.

FEAR

Question: What is Fear?

Fear is a feeling of anxiety and agitation caused by the presence or nearness of danger, evil, pain etc...; timidity; dread; terror; fright; apprehension ... awe ... a feeling of uneasiness.[4] Regardless, it is something that every human being experiences at some level like it or not, admit it or not. And, as stated earlier, we may again, get "emotionally hijacked."

Where does fear come from? Do issues from the past (often imposed on us at the time) or the concern about something that has not yet materialized prevent us from moving forward or being still in the moment? In true living and learning mode, there is no time for fear. We are too busy living in the moment, ensuring our assumptions and perspectives do not create fear that is artificial and unnecessary.

With everything to be discussed and considered, remember that fear is not always bad. Whether a feeling of minor apprehension or absolute terror, fear helps us make associations that protects us from harm. Fear learning is quick, powerful and long lasting. If we think back to our childhood, chances are good that within our earliest memory are events colored by fear. What experiences of fear can we remember that still affect us today? To explore this further, lets take a look at "roots" and "branches".

Metaphorically, "roots" are our set of negative default behaviors. For example, John withdraws as a result of his wife repeatedly telling him to take out the trash. Withdrawing is a "root" default behavior for John. Such default behavior will recur until it is addressed, in a loving and learning way, with plenty of repetition. "Root" causes can be fear, anger, control, emotional reactions, and shame. Additionally, guilt is a negative default behavior many people will often admit to experiencing.

The effects of acting out our negative default behaviors can be identified as "branches". Think of the example referenced: John withdraws when Mary tells him to take out the trash. Mary interprets his body language and withdrawing energy, and she storms out angry. John's "branch" effects have helped to trigger Mary's "root" causes, including anger.

Our negative default behaviors are made up of our past experiences but appear in the present and will continue to appear during all types of personal and professional experiences for the rest of our lives. Negative default behaviors contribute to keeping people stuck. Simply acknowledging their presence can become an indicator light telling us that we need to revisit our perception, responses and the potential consequences, creating an opportunity for transformation.

How many times a day do we turn over the control of our lives to those negatives "root" causes, sabotaging our life decisions, big and small?

Who would we be if we were not afraid?

We live in a fear-based society. Think about the products we are sold — tires to protect babies, deodorant to keep us from being offensive, makeup to take away imperfections, the list goes on and on. Consider how many advertisements in this society try to get us to be afraid of something in order to see more value in their product. Unfortunately in the U.S., that mentality has permeated our collective unconscious. We walk around with a generalized sense of fear; a fear of reflection.

What kind of fears do people face? After countless brainstorms and introspective sessions with many people, we believe the following represent many people's common fears:

Rejection • **Public speaking** • *Disapproval* • **Taking airplane trips**
Not meeting expectations • **Dogs** • **Darkness**
Seeing someone bleed • **Test taking** • **Dentists, doctors and hospitals**
Making mistakes • *People displaying anger* • **Injections** • **Spiders**
Being late • **Drowning** • **Dying young** • **Police** • **Growing Old Alone**

While many would think that spiders or needles or dogs would dominate the list, consider the ones that resonate with internal conflict and how common they are with people in our society…notice the ones in italics all relate to the fear of being judged. We fear being judged because we do not want to have to explain ourselves or measure up to someone else's arbitrary, personal standards that in fact, may have huge consequences on our lives happiness.

Consider this: Fear is a choice. Are we living in the moment and feeling afraid of what is actually taking place in our lives, or are we consumed by rules we have made up about a possible or potential situation that has not even surfaced yet? How often do people stress themselves out, some to the point of physical detriment, merely in the anticipation of an event or potential situation? When the event happens and goes smoothly it indicates that the original fear and stress was merely a waste and a strain on our mind and body.

Consider this: Fear inhibits our ability to learn. How often do we let fear get in the way of meeting someone new, trying a new food, changing a standard way of doing something, changing a professional career, standing up for our individual rights, or admitting wrongdoing? When someone truly believes he or she is in a life-long learning mode, there is no such thing as failure, even in the face of risks for which we must build our own safety net.

Consider this: Fear serves no purpose other than to create chaos and slow us down, especially fear of something that cannot harm us. This has been described as delusions—distorted ways of looking at ourselves and the world around us. Being in the moment, therefore, is a clear indicator that we have become the masters of our minds, rather than having our minds master us.

Fear is a conditioned response, related to physiological mechanisms present in all animals, the technicalities of which are only now being revealed. We know that certain parts of the mind are tasked with managing different fear responses—crying, freeze instinct, violent aggressive posturing, increased heart rate and breathing, etc.

We know that certain brain chemistry impacts the way this system is regulated and that our genetics are involved. But we also know through studies and personal experience that simply thinking differently and relating differently with the object of our fear can influence the triggering of these primitive brain systems. In other words, studies suggest that while the mechanics of our physiology are natural and instinctive, the act of overriding these systems is a learned, conditioned response.

Someone once told us that this inner voice, the part of us that interprets our physical response to a stimulus and decides that the worst will happen is not our fear. It is the part of us that is the willing victim of fear. It is a part of our subconscious that we create and that reinforces and nurtures our fear of a particular thing.

The physical vibrations we interpret as fear can apply to a variety of situations; however, the sensations are always the same. Our system starts to get wound up, our breathing speeds up as our pulse increases and we may even begin to shake.

The difference between fear and excitement is then, only, that we have unconsciously interpreted otherwise meaningless information to mean that the worst will happen.

How to Deal with Fear

Steps to take:
1. If possible, plan, prepare and increase our knowledge
2. Face it. Breathe.
3. Acknowledge the ongoing physiological changes.
4. Try not to associate the fear to an upcoming situation and separate the real fear from the imagined fear.
5. Replace it with learning, curiosity, risk taking (our reality test is, "What would happen if it came true?")
6. Remind ourselves that the experience will end before long.
7. Incorporate the information for transformation. True learning mode means failure cannot exist.
8. Repeat the cycle and strive for new things now that we have moved past old fears.

From Theory to Practice

1. A woman had a fear of dogs. *(Acknowledge it.)*
2. She spent five minutes a day visualizing positive thoughts about walking with 6 dogs. *(Face it.)*
3. Then she contacted three friends who owned dogs and asked them for the opportunity to walk their dogs. *(Try not to associate fear to an upcoming situation.)*
4. Inviting the dog owners to accompany her at first, she walked each of the three dogs, three additional times, solo. *(Replace it with learning, curiosity and risk taking.)*
5. She realized she was not afraid of dogs at all. In fact, she never had a dog because this was her mother's fear. *(Incorporate the information for transformation!)*
6. She looked to conquer new fears because she realized that she could control the outcome and that this, like other conflicts, was her choice. *(In true learning mode, failure cannot exist.)*

Our Challenge

Brainstorm all of the things that we are afraid of in this life. Do not share the list with anyone, if desired. Identify the fear on the list that would be the easiest to overcome. Create a plan to overcome this fear (visualize – strategize – actualize – realize). After completing this task, realize how much more control we have over our lives and our ability to create change.

The two individuals below affected the United States in their own way, took their own risks and helped the country learn more about itself in times of crisis. It does not matter whether we agree with either politically; the question is do we believe their understanding of fear can help us?

"We must do the things we think we cannot."
— ELEANOR ROOSEVELT

"The only thing we have to fear is, fear itself."
— FRANKLIN D. ROOSEVELT

---

4 New World Dictionary of the American Language, 2nd edition, "Fear," Simon and Schuster, Tree of Knowledge, New York, NY, 1984, p. 511.

"Sanity is not how well I can hide my anger; it is having no need to react to people, places, and things by becoming angry."
— OVER EATERS ANONYMOUS

VII.

A.N.G.E.R.

Question: What is Anger?

Anger is "an emotional state that varies in intensity from mild irritation to intense fury and rage," says Charles Spielberger, PhD. in a brochure published by the American Psychological Association.[5]

Often there are mental and biological changes. If we get mad, our heart rate, blood pressure, adrenaline levels and energy hormones all start to rise. Anger comes from deep inside and can take many forms, especially that which has been suppressed.

When someone is using anger as a survival tool, crutch or implement of control, they may become negative, quick-fused, judgmental, disapproving, passively resistant, resentful, and uncooperative, use cynical humor, and/or may be unsympathetic, irritable, jealous, unforgiving and/or argumentative. (Before moving on, we must ask ourselves if some of these behaviors even subtly apply to us. The anger will not go away until we explore it, as painful as that may be. But it is worth the short term pain to get long term gain).

Anger can be such a powerful force in our lives that we take it out on ourselves, physically. When we get really angry (or fearful) we must understand that the body is going through something known as an adrenaline dump. When the body senses anger or aggression, it receives a large shot of adrenaline. While this is normal, it often happens without us knowing it, feeling it, or preparing ourselves to deal with it. The impact of the adrenaline dump cannot be stopped by even most experienced conflict masters. So many people choose to suppress it instead. In doing so, they internalize the anger and will often project or transfer it onto other people in the form of outward judgments, sarcasm, put downs and maybe even violence.

When we are angry we often fail to comprehend the truth regarding the real source of the emotion. The truth, however, is that the initial agitation was only the scab to an internal pain that is often much deeper in our own lives. We need to consider more than the event that took us to that place.

The situation that causes anger is merely a breaking point, opening us to a deeper, unresolved issue. Whether we like it or not, that pain may be a reflection of an unmet childhood need, a pressing issue that we are not dealing with beyond the subconscious mind or something that we have been dreading or painfully wrestling with during our waking hours.

Accessing Negativity Grounded in an Emotional Response

Consider the acronym A.N.G.E.R. (for: Accessing Negativity Grounded in an Emotional Response) and use it as an indicator light when feelings of anger emerge. Internalizing anger may not be the best option. When the light goes off, this will tell us that we need to take more time to respond, behave or speak. If we do not, we are likely to say or do something that will have negative consequences, many of which we did not consider.

Managing our anger can reduce the associated emotional feelings and physiological stimulation most often detrimental to the situation or the relationships involved. A key to anger management is the core belief that we cannot change other people, their behaviors or statements. We can only control our responses to them.

Another key is to know what to do with ourselves when anger arises—to find calm. In this state we can control our internal responses and transition to logic and the ability to express ourselves. Eventually we will be able to prevent the destructive feelings anger creates within us and we often act on.

How to Deal with Our Anger

Steps to take:
1. Limit exposure to people and behaviors that may activate our anger.
2. Mentally recognize anger, identify feelings and don't react.

3. Breathe from the gut!
4. Whisper, "Relax." in our head (count, do something that works to reduce our heart rate, breathing and tone of voice).
5. Logically consider, visualize and choose from many behaviors.
6. Change our environment (we may want to reverse with #4).
7. Consider long term life changes such as mediation, yoga or physical workouts to help slow down our internal motor.

From Theory to Practice

Scott returned home late from a business trip, having had multiple flight delays. He found an urgent e-mail from his colleague requesting he post a project report "before end of that business day" to their Corporate Vice President.

1. Instantly he was consumed by rage. "Didn't he get my voice message that I was delayed at the airport? Couldn't he have handled this!!?" *(Mentally recognize anger.)*
2. *(Breathe from the gut.)*
3. *(Whisper "relax" in our head.)*
4. Scott knew he was the project manager and ultimately responsible for everything that happened. He thought about three different ways the problem could be handled to everyone's satisfaction. *(Logically choose from many behaviors.)*
5. He picked up his laptop, cell phone and project notes and relocated to the local coffee shop to begin taking the required steps for the desired outcome. *(Change our environment.)*

Our Challenge

Like the Vikings, where on their ships each individual was responsible for his own oar, take Ownership, Accountability and Responsibility for our own anger (OAR)!

"No one but ourselves can make us angry. Amongst the choices, it is an emotion we choose ourselves and, ultimately, pay for ourselves."
                              – UNKNOWN

Anger can also be linked back to fear and our next topic, control. Consider the last time we were angry at someone, even if we were right. Ask ourselves some questions about that situation:

1. Am I afraid that he/she won't understand me?
2. Am I afraid that I will be judged?
3. Am I afraid that I won't get what I want?
4. Am I afraid that I won't get what I need?
5. Am I afraid that I will be controlled?

"He who angers you conquers you."
– ELIZABETH KENNY

"Take the power to control your own life. No one else can do it for you.
Take the power to make your life happy."
– SUSAN POLIS SHULTZ

VIII.

CONTROL

Question: What is Control?

Control is when someone else attempts to exercise power, influence or authority over us (subtly or overtly, for small or important issues), whether it is to faintly adjust, judge, regulate, argue, check, provide unsolicited feedback or even try to restrain us from doing something we have chosen, good or bad, right or wrong.

We experience control every day of our lives. Whether it is driving the speed limit, choosing our destiny or what to have for lunch, we make decisions every day based on control.

This may be the single most important ingredient in the F.A.C.T.S. acronym. If we watch an infant playing on the ground, looking to get into something she shouldn't, watch what happens when she is picked up and placed in the stroller. Most children we know go through a period where they truly fight being moved without their consent. They kick, squirm, cry, pout and slam their fists. Potentially, we all learn at a very early age to fight back when we feel that anyone is trying to control us.

Individuals in conflict often digress back to these behaviors and reflect their inner child. As adults, we have vast vocabularies with which to express ourselves. Yet we often find ourselves in struggles where both parties are really dressing up basic, childlike power and control situations.

Even an internalized, false belief around control issues is enough to cause a major fiasco. When we get angry, we attempt to control everything. Think of a funnel. When we are angry, behaviors and communication all funnel to control issues.

A Deeper Look

The Locus of Control refers to our ability to internally place the power of personal influence—how we feel about ourselves and others—in our own hands or others.[6] It can be external or internal. If it's external, we are subject to being controlled by others.

The Internal Locus of Control exists when we place the control of our personal self-approval, self-recognition, self-acceptance, self-reinforcement, and self-affirmation of worth into our own hands. On the other side, External Locus of Control exists when we are willing to give other people, places, and things the power to influence our feelings about ourselves.[7]

The Internal Locus of Control places energy and self-affirmation, acceptance, recognition, approval in our own hands.[8] It is up to us to develop our own self-love and self-worth. We can feel valuable, creative, smart, capable and skilled. We do not let those feelings be controlled by others. We are ultimately responsible for our own behaviors, thoughts and feelings.

Looking Outside Ourselves

Rotter describes the External Locus of Control as giving other people, places, and things the power to influence our feelings about ourselves. It is related to conflicts that are between us and other people.[9]

Interestingly enough, most of the external conflict that we blame on others—stupidity, madness or incompetence—comes back to hurt us internally. We then create new external conflict with others in our lives. Remember the story of the man who got yelled at by his boss, went home and hit his wife, who smacked the kid, who kicked the dog? This was nothing more than a cycle of internal-external conflicts repeating and regenerating all over again, like a violent game of whisper down the lane. Who did the man blame for how he was feeling about himself?

The first step of control is self-control, and that comes from within. One way to begin to demonstrate self control is to work and dialogue with others more successfully. Consider a simple paradigm: To vs. With. How are these words used to control or demonstrate power? Do we speak to our colleagues or with them? Do we speak to our family or do we speak with them? Consider how "To" and "With" create very different dynamics.

"To" promotes:
- Justification
- Self-centered behavior
- Direction
- Control
- Defined boundaries
- Resentment

The "With" requires and allows:
- Co-active behavior
- Ambiguity
- Cooperation and co-activity
- Desired mutual objectives
- Independent thinking
- Co-authorship
- Potential consensus and positive results as a result of positive relationship

In order to move beyond our issues of control, we must work with ourselves and others every day of our lives. Control has a lot to do with who decides our outcomes.

How to Overcome Control Issues

Steps to take:
1. Recognize the power struggle.
2. Relinquish power. Simply let go of the desire to be right.
3. Move into the experience and out of expectation.
4. Understand the upcoming cause and effect and take responsibility for our decision and consequences.
5. Understand physiological changes and avoid power assertion and one-upmanship.
6. Express empathy, sensitivity and the belief in a solution.
7. Have courage to create the opportunity for a perspective change,

dynamic shift or an outcome that was different than the one we had before feeling like we were being controlled.

From Theory to Practice

1. Sylvia, a successful attorney, suffered from an emotionally charged childhood message from her mother (*Recognize the power struggle.*) "You are stupid, you are a coward, and your life will never amount to anything." (*Recognize the message.*)
2. At age 35, Sylvia decided she could not endure this suffering anymore. (*Relinquish power—simply let go.*)
3. Her rise to professional excellence in her chosen field inspired her to look at the rest of her life. (*Move into the experience and out of the expectation.*)
4. For years she had convinced herself her professional excellence would bridge any and all gaps. She then realized what she had overlooked— health threatening weight gain which led to an unfulfilled desire to attract a marriageable partner. (*Understand cause and effect.*)
5. Shifting her perspective from her mother's message to her own, "I am smart, I am resourceful, I can change anything." (*Recognize the physiological changes.*)
6. Sylvia immediately enrolled in a weight management program. (*Express belief in the solution.*)
7. She also joined a health club and started accepting invitations to meet and join others. (*Have the courage to create opportunity based on her new, self controlled perspective.*)

Our Challenge

The challenge for ourselves is to listen and trust ourselves even more. This trust, deeply entrenched in our beings, is always available to us when we look. We simply need to know and believe that. Then, we are truly taking control of our own outcomes in every aspect of our lives. The next time we have an important decision to make, trust ourselves to detach from the desired results and simply do what needs to be done. The outcome will be achieved.

"Ultimately, the only power to which man should aspire
is that which he exercises over himself."
— ELIE WIESEL

6 Julian Rotter, "The Social Learning Theory of Julian B. Rotter," California State
  University, Fullerton Department of Psychology, September 11, 2005,
  <http://psych.fullerton.edu/jmearns/rotter.htm> (July 26, 2006).
7 Ibid.
8 Ibid.
9 Ibid.

"If passion drives you,
let reason hold the reins"
– Benjamin Franklin

IX.

TIMING

Question: What is Timing?

One aspect of timing is the way we react or respond to incoming words or behaviors from the outside world. It is important to note that we live in a society that is very reactive and fearful. People often feel defensive. Remember, no one likes to be judged or forced to explain why they did or did not do something.

The distinction between reacting and responding is critical. Essentially, most of us react because we have not trained our brain to slow down. When we slow down in conflict, our brain has time to become flooded with options. This means we are actively choosing a response, rather than allowing an internal, emotional or physical change to dictate how we will speak or behave (i.e., react).

Reacting is a sudden, immediate internal physical and emotional response and possibly an external come back given with little thought, lots of emotion and, quite often, no consideration of how it will affect others, including ourselves.

Responding means to slow down, select a path, decision or behavior while considering the action itself, the people affected and the possible consequences.

Emotional reactions are, in reality, changes to our internal chemistry, i.e. changes in blood pressure, heart rate, hormone and chemical secretions, and much more. Essentially, we are feeling our bodies change quickly and we don't like it. After we experience these types of reactions over time, we label them based upon our understanding of the context of the situation.

Think about this simply. Do we often get a similar physical response when we experience these emotions: *Fear, Anxiety, Elation, Frustration, Sorrow, Joy?*

Reptilian REACTion

The Reptilian REACTion describes how humans respond automatically to positive or negative events without consciously thinking about the consequences. It is grounded in emotion, not logic. Derived from the theory of the reptilian brain, this teaching principle describes the sequence of events in a cause and effect relationship. It claims that the primitive (reptilian) part of the brain controls lust, fear, hate and love. When we REACT, we are actually operating with this primitive part, using emotion over logic and reason.

Reptiles and other animals do this instinctively. So do people who have not been taught to slow down and consider their actions and consequences, both immediate and long term. Usually the choice of reactive behavior is not a conscious choice at all. Rather, it is a reaction that perpetuates negativity and often creates a cycle of conflict that spirals out of control.

People often resort to this behavior when their coping skills are limited or they cannot see other options. They stick with the approaches that they are most comfortable with and experienced in using. But once they are consciously aware of how they feel, they can make a better choice.

While it is easy to believe that we are reacting to the events in our lives, remember, our feelings in the moment are related to our immediate, internalized interpretations and preconceived notions about the event. Therefore, the way we interpret events will often dictate our response or Reptilian REACTion.

How to avoid reacting and control decision making

1. Understand our own emotions.
   - Understand the causes of our feelings.
   - Become aware of our hot buttons.
   - Develop frustration tolerance.
   - Strengthen our self concept, and reduce our dependence on external validation.
2. Recognize the isolated action.
3. Stop—DO NOT REACT—and breathe.
   - Avoid thinking in terms of extremes.

- Avoid believing that our perspective is the only one that exists.
- Do not over generalize or blow things out of proportion.
- Do not personalize the entire conflict.
- Do not allow this experience to overshadow our successes.
4. Ask ourselves if it is possible that we misinterpreted what they said, or they misinterpreted us.
5. Step into the space of "now."
6. Acknowledge options, impact, and consequences. (What are my options for expressing my feelings?)
7. Select a response using logic over emotion.
8. Or stated another way…
   - Identify the action or behavior.
   - Step willingly and knowingly into the space.
   - Identify potential responses.
   - Identify the consequences and impact of each option.
   - Knowingly choose a response based upon a conscious decision.

From Theory to Practice

1. Without any warning Michelle's husband snapped at her about something related to an argument the day before. (*Recognize the action.*)
2. Before speaking, she decided to wait. (*Do not react, step willingly into the space.*)
3. She considered her response. She could yell, turn away, cry, fight, etc. (*Identify potential responses and acknowledge options, impact, and consequences.*)
4. In a calm manner she responded with, "It sounds like you have feelings about yesterday's discussion. If we can speak respectfully to each other, I would be happy to listen to what is on your mind." (*Knowingly choose a response based upon a conscious decision.*)
5. (*Select a response using logic over emotion.*)

Our Challenge

Try to remove the word "but" from our reflective listening vocabulary. Remember that when we say the word "but," we effectively negate everything said by the speaker up to that point. Re-state what we heard and end the sentence, rather than saying, "but, what I believe is." Also remember, "but" can be seen as directive and manipulative, neither of which perpetuates a problem solving environment or one that is conducive to communication or conflict management.

"Most of us don't spend any time knowing ourselves.
We just keep reacting."
– Jewel Kilcher

"If our fellow men could be aware of our opinions about them, love, friendship, and devotion would be forever erased from the dictionaries; and if we had the courage to confront the doubts we timidly conceive about ourselves, none of us would utter an 'I' without shame."
— EMILE M. CIORAN

X.

SHAME

Question: What is Shame?

Shame includes:
Feelings of embarrassment, blame and responsibility for negative circumstances that have befallen yourself or others. Feelings of regret for your real or imagined misdeeds, both past and present. Sense of remorse for thoughts, feelings, or attitudes that were or are negative, uncomplimentary, or non-accepting concerning yourself or others. Feelings of obligation for not pleasing, not helping, or not placating another. Feelings of bewilderment and lack of balance for not responding to a situation in the "correct way".[10]

Remember a red light that turned green and we didn't step on the gas peddle fast enough? *Honk! Honk! Honk!* Some people feel shame. "Oops, sorry, I should have gone." Shame results when we instantly judge ourselves.

There are many causes for shame, and we often allow it to become a major obstacle in our lives. Shame can result from a fear of rejection, depression, irrational beliefs, and denial of past hurts, victimization or even the silent withdrawal of anger. Shame represents some of the deepest forms of vulnerability, insecurity and fear of rejection.

How do we respond to shame?

Examine how the "Elements of Shame" reflect the major responses to shame in our lives. While some of these overlap, use this to understand common responses.

1. **Isolate**: Shame results when we separate ourselves from others and withdraw from feelings or a situation.
2. **Hostile to Self**: Masochistic behavior involves putting ourselves down. Some individuals will actually hurt themselves physically.
3. **Escape**: To do things to sidetrack ourselves from the realities we face, either through denunciation, avoidance or by using drugs and alcohol as a way to flee.
4. **Hostile to Others**: Involves lashing out verbally or physically, being outwardly confrontational, blaming the victim or transforming our shame into something about the other person we can judge, criticize or blame.

How to Overcome Shame

Steps to take:
1. Acknowledge root causes in our lives before isolated situations happen.
2. When an incident happens, notice the physical reaction we may have to shame.
3. Recognize the role of shame.
4. Redefine our problem with the absence of shame.
5. Smile and give the problem back.

From Theory to Practice

Consider the "red light" situation mentioned at the start of the chapter. How would we apply the steps? For example,

1. Recognize that we were daydreaming. (*Acknowledge root cause.*)
2. Don't judge ourselves. (*Recognize the role of shame.*)
3. Understand that our timeline is different than others. (*Re-define the problem with the absence of shame.*)
4. Give back the shame with a smile and a sincere wave of apology. (*Give the problem back.*)

Our Challenge

Next time we find ourselves at a red light that switches to green and a honk blares from behind, try to remember the difference between reacting and responding. Try to remember that we have not made a mistake, and we do not need to defend ourselves with words or actions. Simply, try to smile and think about how this event will not impact our day, other than to be seen as a reward to our inner selves and personal growth.

"I never wonder to see men wicked,
but I often wonder to see them not ashamed."
– JONATHAN SWIFT

"History is the only car
without a reverse."
– WINSTON CHURCHILL

XI.

CONCLUSION

As Winston Churchill's quote implies, we believe that regardless of what action or lack of action an individual, organization or business has taken, prior to reading this, time is moving forward. The moment for self realization and improvement is now. Moreover, here now are the issues to improve our lives by reducing conflict in and around us even though they were never discussed in our parental discussions, teacher lesson plans or religious teachings.

The bottom line? This "stuff" isn't easy. The only way to get better at dealing with F.A.C.T.S., or conflict in our lives, is to practice doing it right, when the inevitable conflict of life meanders its way into our daily lives. It is easy to read a book, and yet another story to translate it to workable tasks and goals that we can accomplish on our own. The key is to get on the path towards self-improvement, acknowledge faults without judgment and work more consciously next time to avoid default behavior and the patterns we have developed over time.

That said, we recommend a life coach or friend that we can share our concerns with on a regular basis. The only way we learn about these issues is to constantly examine our ways of speaking and behaving, how we have treated other people and how we respond to the things that happen in our lives. Our ability to recognize our own "stuff" and not take it out on others is a daily event. We have a choice. We can seek a better outcome, or we can be satisfied living beneath our potential for happiness, growth and the personal and professional nirvana we all crave.

When we are truly paying attention to our own behavior, we can recognize conflict. And like a stone thrown in the water producing ripples, there will be a cause and potentially long lasting impact. Where did that stone originate?

Where was it before it hit the water? A true, often painful, look within can reveal not only the personal or professional stone, but its true origin. How well do we listen to our own lives, our higher selves so to speak, and step back? We all walk around with a bag of stones. Who do we throw them at when we do not feel good or completely comfortable with ourselves?

"Your real security is yourself. You know you can do it,
and they can't ever take that away from you."
— MAE WEST

"Our deepest fear is not that we are inadequate.
It is our light, not our darkness, that most frightens us.
We ask ourselves, who am I to be brilliant, gorgeous, talented and fabulous?
Actually, who are you not to be?"
– MARIANNE WILLIAMSON

Works Cited/Consulted

Print:

Fischer, Robert, William Ury, and Patton, Bruce, Getting to Yes: Negotiating Agreement without Giving In, Penguin Group, New York, 1981.

New World Dictionary of the American Language, 2nd edition, "Fear," Simon and Schuster, Tree of Knowledge, New York, 1984.

Online:

International Institute for Restorative Practices, "What is Restorative Practices," International Institute for Restorative Practices, n.d., <http://www.restorativepractices.org/library/whatisrp.html>, Jul 26, 2006.

McManamy, John, "Anger and Depression in Bipolar Disorder," McMan's Depression and Bipolar Web, n.d., <http://www.mcmanweb.com/anger.htm> (July 26, 2006).

Messina, James J., Ph.D., "Growing Down: Tools for Healing the Inner Child Letting Go of Shame and Guilt," Coping.org, n.d., <http://www.coping.org/innerhealing/shame.htm> 2006.

Panic-attacks.co.uk, "Part 5: The Brain and Panic Attacks: Emotional Hijacking," The Panic Attack Prevention Program, 2001-2006, <http://www.panic-attacks.co.uk/panic_attacks_5.htm /> July 26, 2006.

Rotter, Julian, "The Social Learning Theory of Julian B. Rotter," California State University, Fullerton Department of Psychology, September 11, 2005, <http://psych.fullerton.edu/jmearns/rotter.htm> (July 26, 2006).

Wordreference.com, "Conflict," Wordreference.com, 2003, <http://www.wordreference.com/definition/conflict/> (July 26, 2006).

Suggested Resources:
www.synergydt.com
www.coachingcenterofreston.com
www.synergydte.com
www.theconflictmaster.com
www.conflictmasters.com
www.kingofconflict.com

"Never doubt that a small group of thoughtful, committed people can change the world. Indeed. It is the only thing that ever has."
– MARGARET MEAD

ABOUT THE AUTHORS

 Dave Gerber is President and Founder of Synergy Development & Training, LLC, an innovative organizational solutions company, specializing in helping businesses, government agencies and schools use conflict to increase performance, revenue and reduce risk. Synergy accomplishes this through specialized training, facilitation, conflict management seminars, professional development and leadership coaching.

Dave is a coach and professional speaker that helps individuals understand the impact of conflict on business, schools, organizations and the government. He specializes in motivating others to increase and actualize their new professional and personal potential.

Dave has a great understanding of how people work, how to expand upon their potential and how to motivate and inspire them to action. He is dedicated to people and relationships and truly enjoys helping diverse work and academic environments prevent, manage and resolve conflict.

He has worked with business owners, managers, employees of all kinds, CEOs, U.S. Military Officers and Supervisors, business development directors, doctors, lawyers, engineers, educators and more in a coaching, training and consulting capacity.

His goal is always to help individuals improve their personal, professional and organizational abilities. His expertise spans the areas of conflict resolution and organizational problem solving, team building, group facilitation, Interest-Based Negotiations, diversity education, communication and beyond. He has hands-on experience working with thousands of training participants and students of all ages, races, backgrounds and ability levels.

Dave received a bachelor's degree in Sociology from Ithaca College (New York), a master's degree in education from St. Joseph's University (Philadelphia) and a Senior Executive Leadership certificate from Georgetown University (Washington, D.C.). He has certificates in Workplace Conflict Processes, Workplace Mediation and Conflict Resolution, Commercial, Federal Workplace and Family Mediation from the Northern Virginia Mediation Service at George Mason. Dave brings 12 years of varied conflict management, teaching, coaching and educator-training experience as well. His passionate and motivating style is contagious.

Pamela Leech is a certified co-active life coach and mentor. After more than 25 years in corporate sales and marketing, Pamela launched Coaching Center of Reston in 2002 to provide a professional coaching opportunity for residents of Northern Virginia and Washington, D.C.

Today that opportunity is global. Pamela provides to individuals and corporations coaching and seminars designed to reconnect each participant with his or her internal guidance system, fostering self-leadership in service of truly living a balanced, happy, fulfilled life. She often says, "Look in the mirror and see a human being of limitless potential."

"Never neglect the little things. Never skimp on that extra effort, that additional few minutes, that soft word of praise or thanks, that delivery of the very best that you can do.
It does not matter what others think, it is of prime importance, however, what you think about you. You can never do your best, which should always be your trademark, if you are cutting corners and shirking responsibilities. You are special. Act it. Never neglect the little things."
— OG MANDINO